For **SADIE, GREYSON,** their
Mommy, and all of our friends
with little ones old(er) and new(er)

www.mascotbooks.com

IN MOMMY'S TUMMY

For more information, please contact:
Mascot Books
620 Herndon Parkway, Suite 320
Herndon, VA 20170
info@mascotbooks.com

Library of Congress Control Number: 2019918363

CPSIA Code: PRT0220A
ISBN-13: 978-1-64543-378-1

Printed in the United States

In Mommy's Tummy

MATTHEW E. BASS

Illustrated by Ashley Bittner

Not too long ago you were in
MOMMY'S TUMMY.

YOU WERE THERE when she was eating, and sleeping, and running.

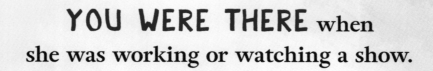

YOU WERE THERE when
she was working or watching a show.

You were there from the first day
you started **TO GROW.**

You went with Mommy wherever she was going. And everyone said that
MOMMY WAS GLOWING.

But at first Mommy wasn't quite sure it was you. Because you were so very small and SO VERY NEW.

Then one day Mommy found out you were
there. And she started to plan all the clothes
YOU WOULD WEAR.

Mommy's tummy got bigger with each passing day.
And she started to plan all the games
YOU WOULD PLAY.

Mommy's family and friends bought her
LOTS OF NICE THINGS. Like your bed,
and your clothes, and your chair, and your swing.

Mommy and Daddy got little pictures of you.
To show your grandparents, aunts, and uncles
IT WAS TRUE.

And at night before bed they talked
about YOUR NAME.

Until finally one day they agreed
on THE SAME.

Sometimes Mommy would say your name and her tummy would **RUMBLE**.

And you'd **KICK**, and you'd **ROLL**, and you'd **PUNCH**, and you'd **TUMBLE!**

Then Daddy would read you a story.
Or two. OR THREE.

And eventually you would
FALL ASLEEP.

Because even when you were
in Mommy's tummy YOU COULD HEAR.

You had a tiny little MOUTH, and
a NOSE, and two EARS...

And ARMS, and LEGS, and
HANDS, and FEET.

You were still very small, but you were
ALMOST COMPLETE.

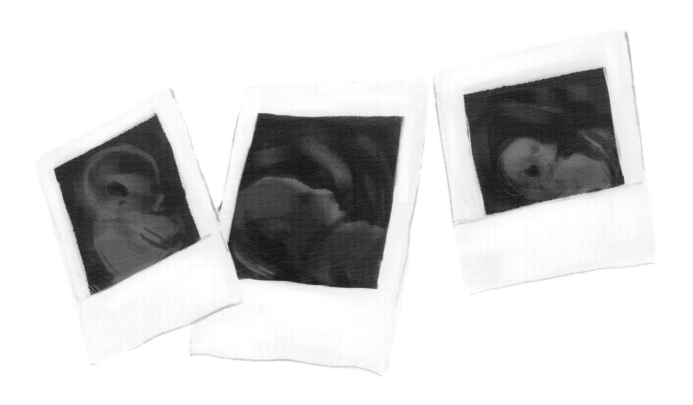

Mommy and Daddy
wondered when you would
ARRIVE.

So they could count FINGERS and
TOES, from one to five.

And the days passed quickly the more
time went by. Mommy and Daddy
couldn't wait to say **"HI!"**

Pretty soon you were too big to stay in
Mommy's tummy. So you told Mommy:
"MOMMY, I'M COMING!"

You said: "Bye bye, MOMMY'S TUMMY!"
Because it was finally time,

For you to come out of Mommy's tummy and open **YOUR EYES**.

AND SO like other baby boys
and baby girls...

You came out of Mommy's tummy to
SAY "HI" TO THE WORLD.

ABOUT THE ILLUSTRATOR

Ashley Bittner spent her childhood in coastal California, and her young adult years in Northern Virginia. She has a love for both the seashore and the countryside. Her inspiration for the artwork in this book stems from old fairy tales and the whimsical cottages of Virginia, along with the deep woods, rolling hills, and fields of flowers native to her county. Ashley started drawing at the age of five, and has pursued art classes at her local college, and also studied under accomplished art masters.

Along with her work in freelance illustration, her hobbies include decorating, arranging flowers, and working with horses. Growing up, the thought of being a children's book illustrator was always appealing to her and she feels that meeting Matthew Bass was a God-given opportunity. She looks forward to illustrating more books in the future, and hopes that this one brings you delight!

ABOUT THE AUTHOR

Matthew E. "Matt" Bass is, among other things (including lawyer, sportsman, and musician), a writer and author. He is also a proud daddy to daughter Sadie and son Greyson, and husband to wife Kelbi. They live in Matt's hometown of Berryville, Virginia. *In Mommy's Tummy* was inspired by a poem Matt wrote after Sadie (his first child) was born in 2016.

The concept for an illustrated children's book came about when Matt happened upon a beautifully illustrated Christmas card accidentally sent to his house by artist/illustrator Ashley Bittner. He eventually figured out that the card was meant for a neighbor, but nevertheless contacted Ashley to see if she would be interested in illustrating for him. Fortunately, she agreed. Matt plans for *In Mommy's Tummy* to be the first of multiple children's books covering a range of themes in the coming years and currently has several projects in various stages of production.

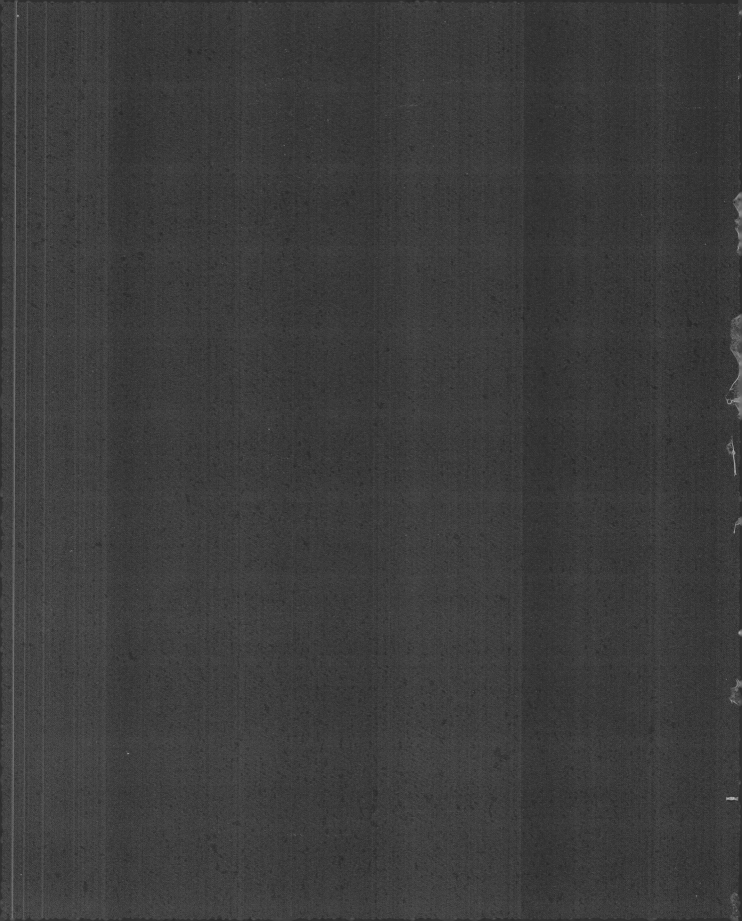